# From 9/11 to a New Year

**vox poetica** Contributor Series 2009

ISBN 978-1-936373-01-7

© 2010 Unbound Content, LLC. All rights retained by the original authors with the exception of first-time anthology rights to distribute this collection. These first-time anthology rights are held by Unbound Content, LLC, and this anthology is published as part of the vox poetica Contributor Series collection. Cover image is owned by Manny Beltran. All other images owned by Unbound Content, LLC. Permission for use requests will be forwarded.

From 9/11 to a New Year
**vox poetica** Contributor Series 2009

With much appreciation to Manny Beltran for his inspired cover art and to the writers for being so generous with their gifts.

In memory of those lost in the attacks of September 11, 2001 and those who lost their lives as a consequence of their involvement in the rescue and recovery efforts following the attacks. The death toll continues to climb.

In 2009, **vox poetica** was launched, and the first year of its existence saw the beginnings of a tradition: the Contributor Series. The poems that appeared in the series were invited via calls for submissions sent only to writers whose work had already been published or accepted for publication at **vox poetica**, the idea being to create a conversation among these talented writers on a particular theme.

The first series was focused on 9/11; for many of the writers it was their first attempt at tackling the subject creatively. The second series coincided with Halloween and centered around the concepts of fright and delight. The third series was meant to explore the ups and downs of new year resolutions. Taken together, the poems of these three series create an artistic, thought-provoking dialogue incorporating a wide range of elements central and peripheral to the named themes.

It is my distinct honor and pleasure to present these first three series, this journey from 9/11 to a new year, in the first of what promises to be a long line of collections of fine work by fine writers on a diverse assortment of topics.

—Annmarie Lockhart, editor

# Table of Contents

## Contributor Series 1: 9/11

Threnody for the Survivors of September 11, 2001, by Ray Sharp ............... 9
September Morn, by Sandra Forte-Nickenig ................................................. 10
Bone Fragments, by Annmarie Lockhart ..................................................... 11
Tuesday Morning Rising, by R Scott DeSena ............................................... 12
The Day We Know as 9/11, by Anna Alpine ................................................ 13
The tv is on at work, by Sarah Endo ............................................................ 14
Afterwards, by Kim Klugh ............................................................................ 15
9/11, by Sharon Poch .................................................................................... 16
New Day, by Gianluca D'Elia ........................................................................ 17
9-12, by Danielle Cross ................................................................................. 18
Remembering that September, by Linda Ardison ....................................... 19
Armageddon 9/11, by Jean McLeod .............................................................. 20
What the tree has seen, by Cassie Premo Steele ......................................... 22

## Contributor Series 2: Candy and Spirits

Table Mountain, Cape Town, by John Lavan .............................................. 25
POEm, by Val B Russell ................................................................................ 26
Trick or Treat With Pets (How My Dog Sees Hallowe'en), by Ken Karrer ...... 29
Trick or Treat, A Cinquain, by Mark Gooch ................................................ 30
Shhhhh ... , by Joan McNerney ..................................................................... 31
Who Kissed My Neck? by Gianluca D'Elia .................................................. 32
Greedy Ghouls, by Karen Schindler ............................................................. 34
Jack's Demise, by Kim Klugh ........................................................................ 35
La Llorona, The Weeping Woman, by Ray Sharp ........................................ 36
Jersey Boys, by Bryan Borland ..................................................................... 38
Days of the Dead, by Cassie Premo Steele ................................................... 39

# Contributor Series 3: Resolution and Resolve

Resolution 2009, by Gianluca D'Elia .................................................................. 41
Unheard, by Chris G Vaillancourt ...................................................................... 42
If I stop to pick up a leaf, by Sarah Endo ......................................................... 44
Homelessness ... it's real, by Jimmi Ware-Phillips ........................................... 45
Recipe for the impossible, by Cassie Premo Steele ........................................ 46
Resolutions, by Eve Hall ....................................................................................... 47
What Dreams Are Made of, by Neil Ellman ..................................................... 48
My Uncertain Life, by James G Piatt ................................................................. 50
Lost Dream, by Joan McNerney ..........................................................................51
Weathering, by Dee Thompson ........................................................................... 52
I dropped it again, by Rae Spencer ....................................................................54
The Silence of Wind, by Kay Middleton ...........................................................56
The Navigators, by Joseph Murphy ...................................................................58

The Contributors .................................................................................................60

Contributor Series 1: 9/11

## Threnody for the Survivors of September 11, 2001
By Ray Sharp

The angel of death flew on silver wings.
Strange solitary birds clad in dark feathers
Tumbled through the bright blue sky.

A blizzard of confetti—scraps of lives
Torn asunder—swirled on air currents stirred
By three thousand souls, or by their absence.

Tall towers slumped and crashed earthward,
Their steel bones and skin of glass melted and
Crushed by the inevitability of gravity that pulls

Us to the grave. Now, eight years hence,
The rescuers who breathed the fine particles
Of pulvered lives are falling to the same rare cancer

I came to know when it took my father two years ago.
Were the silent seeds of sickness already
Planted in him so far away on that fateful day?

I scattered my father's ashes on a desert hilltop
To which I may never return. In wind and rain
And blazing heat they will join with the soil

That gives life anew. In living there comes pain
And grief, but in death may we find comfort.
Ashes to ashes, dust to dust.

**vox poetica**

**September Morn**
By Sandra Forte-Nickenig

In the unspoiled country
time stops
for a bather in the dawn
of a new day.
Across the river
time tunelessly ticks in the city.
A bather steps onto a blue bath mat
A child packs snacks in his Batman bag
A father sips a second cup of coffee
A mother sighs as her child climbs the yellow school bus
A teacher takes attendance as students whisper
A dog lifts a leg on his favorite hydrant
A restaurant worker switches the sign to open
A street washer cleans the gutters on Wall Street
A firefighter greets a coworker at Engine Company 12

A worker presses the button for the 102nd floor
A plane flies through tower number 2
The clock stops at 8:45.
Back in the unspoiled country
the bather weeps.
Innocence drowns.

**Bone Fragments**
By Annmarie Lockhart

pool-bottom blue sky
gone black with soul dust,
and the air reeked of wreckage
'til the rains came in late October

poster parade of the missing
pasted up on impromptu prayer walls
that used to be chain-link fences
or walls or trees or windows

in the immediate of the falldown
no water, no power
no cell phone towers
standing; all gone dead

but the shock
and the shock
and the shock
of the shatter still reverberates

last calls and final falls
as the place that was
became the place that is
a sacred, soundless shrine of sky-strewn souls

**vox poetica**

### Tuesday Morning Rising
By R Scott DeSena

Tuesday morning rising
Two shadows
Turnpike
Turn my mind to stone
Traffic screaming to a halt
Chills crawling to the bone.

Fires for days
Billowing clouds
Smoke-filled ash
Filled with lost souls
Crying for salvation
A new terror unfolds.

We will never be the same
Still looking for excuses
Still looking for blame
We are all losers
In a terrorist game.

Never forget the images
Never forget the tears
Never forget the innocent
Not in a million years.

**The Day We Know as 9/11**
By Anna Alpine

It was a day of new beginnings.
My daughter started preschool
and my son was off to first grade.
It was a day of heavenly beauty.
The sky was bright blue with soft clouds
and the sun warmed my skin.
It was a day of horror.
Lives lost and hearts shattered.
It was a day of lost innocence.
We are no longer safe.

**The tv is on at work**
By Sarah Endo

the tv is on at work—
I see people tumble in the sky

are they still alive
air is soft, isn't it

the tv is on at work, but
can we please go home

be with people we love
every instant

## Afterwards
By Kim Klugh

the sun still chases
the moon from the sky
leaves still curl then drift
from the tree like flakes of soot
floating to the ground
sparrows gather and fend at the feeder
for perching rights or dip their beaks
to sip from the birdbath
towels from the dryer are warm
in my hand
the phone still rings

I remind my stunned children
we are alive
we have purpose
though altered we are not
completely shattered
we must heal—it is our duty
to become the messengers
for those who can no longer sing
or speak for themselves
with God's grace we must
go on claiming wisdom
and courage as our allies

to do any less
is to grant victory to evil

**vox poetica**

### 9/11
By Sharon Poch

Brittle brown days of autumn
once lush with harvest scent
now smell of
ash, cinders, human flesh

One plane, then a second
slice through the innocent towers
and they fall, screaming
into September earth

A bewildered blue sky
blinks away tears of smoke
unaware that the world
is forever changed

**New Day**
By Gianluca D'Elia

This day still stays on my mind
Since the moment it occurred
No day is such a tragedy
A catastrophe for my native land
A loss to my own family
And a day that I once lied,
"Everything will be alright,"
When in my heart, I was really scared.

At night the news still releases stories
As I cry myself to sleep
And blow out the dying flame of peacefulness
Set aside the past for tonight
A new day's coming
I close my eyes
And let tomorrow shine.

*The writer, who was attending preschool on 9/11, dedicates this poem to the loving memory of his cousin, Joseph O Pick, who died in the disaster, and to all those who mourn.*

**vox poetica**

### 9-12
By Danielle Cross

Ashes.
To ashes
we pour our tears,
sculpt familiar faces with frantic
hands, paint them with bleeding hearts.
Color has drained from this world, this gray canvas reflecting
our hope,
our futility.
We must be artists now, and we carry on, creating frescoes
from the ground,
from metal
feather dust. To dust remaining
devoted, even now
as we breathe
and it scatters
to the wind.

*The writer dedicates this poem to the loving memory of her husband's cousin, Timmy, who died in the disaster, and to all those who mourn.*

**Remembering That September**
By Linda Ardison

They leap and fall like rag dolls,
Splay out onto the pavement.
There's no one to catch them
Or to snatch the others
From the glowing Staircase B,
No one to blow the white ash
Off the world, once smoke-swirl
Billows through the screaming streets
Until all feet are white with new snow;
Over the East River, streams of clean
Air clarify the sky, but no planes fly,
Except in Washington, and Shanksville,
Plummeting to earth like silver toys—
A day made perfect by September sun
Before the running crowd cries out.
The twin towers flatten like the blocks
A small boy stacks, then sweeps
His hand through in a power rage.

### Armageddon 9/11
By Jean McLeod

The golems bring warships to worship.
        The priests pretend they believe.
The heathens heap coal on the altar.
        A magician pulls fire from his sleeve.

Clowns run the liturgy at high mass
        sycophants bay at the moon.
The terrorists paint faces on airplanes
        shamans fall faint in a swoon.

The sinners and saints wear red cowls
        it's hard to tell who is who.
The truth filters through filthy windows
        the lies and falsehoods shine true.

Fires in the sky à la Tennyson
        fling flames with a sulfurous smell
smoke billows up through the heavens
        and clouds reflect visions of hell.

Lovers become incandescent
        and leave their fiery path
to fighters and screamers and schemers
        who bake in a puddle of wrath.

## From 9/11 to a New Year

The whole world stops in its spinning
        continents slip off their plates.
The team that was losing is winning
        enemies abandon debates.

The world stews and festers with anger.
        Our galaxy expands on its own.
Suns explode without warning
        and earth gives up life with a groan.

vox poetica

**What the tree has seen**
By Cassie Premo Steele

In the middle of a city park
women gather with each other
near an ancient magic tree
and sing of what the tree has seen.

In the south, a woman sings of eyes
stabbed open, and of other eyes sewn shut,
while beneath the morning sky of blue,
children played on swings and pigeons cooed.

No one moved when in the north a woman
screamed, her teeth and tongue torn wide,
her grey tone rising 'til it turned to stone
and, wailing, fell upon the ground nearby.

In the west, a woman kept a constant rhythm,
laying bare hands against the wood,
with heavy patience, as only a mother,
mourning her weaning child, could.

Still in the east there stands an ancient woman,
who calls upon the spirit with upraised hands
of five-fingered yellow leaves in autumn light.
She prays to bring back breath to all those
still sleeping, or dead, or not quite,
as day descends and turns the tree to night.

From 9/11 to a New Year

Moonlit, the women stand in silence
and raise a toast to all the tree has seen.
They are drunk in honor of her memory,
what makes possible the songs they sing.

Contributor Series 2: Candy and Spirits

From 9/11 to a New Year

### Table Mountain, Cape Town
By John Lavan

Your uphill path isn't haunted—even
baseball caps on hikers comfort you

until an unusualness

when something warm and bony
gets on my back, reaches and squeezes
my frightened wrist until
I let go,
alarmed, of my chocolate
bar and the skeleton creature whoops and
springs baboon
to the fallen sweet and grinningly turns,
devours it in dust,

clicking

and there's horror
isn't there?
when you panic
suddenly
gotten onto
from behind
by a grinning
gripping
carcass
silently
from behind

isn't there?

## POEm
### By Val B Russell

The evening crept into my room
Beneath the fullness of the moon
The hour struck just ten that night
As I wrote by candlelight
I'd heard it said once long ago
Its flame invoked the soul of Poe
You see it was my secret dream
To outdo Poe and write a scream
Something wicked to delight
A story of horrific fright
As I tapped the keys to tell my tale
My laptop announced a new e-mail
I looked at who the note was from
Apparently it was from "no one"!
Out loud I said "this cannot be
Someone must be spamming me"
I poised my hand and pushed delete
An action I would soon repeat
Within no time I got some more
First twenty-nine, then forty-four
Finally the spamming ceased
My frenzied fingers felt released
Just as I sat back and sighed
My calm repose was soon denied
The room became as cold as ice
I saw my breath and shivered twice
My laptop screen became bright blue
A truly terrorizing hue
I couldn't move or close my mouth

My stomach churned, my guts went south
When suddenly a face appeared
My laptop screen a frame of fear
At first it looked an eerie glow
Then became the face of Poe!
You can imagine my surprise to see
The illustrious Poe gazing back at me
Within no time his mouth did speak
His face was gaunt and his eyes were bleak
"I plead, don't tell me, nevermore,
For you are still my sweet Lenore
Reborn as one called Annmarie
Your new name matters not to me!"
I felt so shocked, my lips were dry
But I could not accept this blatant lie
"I am not your sweet Lenore!
You don't belong here anymore"
Poe's face turned grim at this remark
His eyes were flashing bits of spark
I blinked as he appeared to me
Beside my chair and touching me
I felt a chill go up my spine
As Poet let out a little whine
"Oh sweet Lenore, you are aware
I've come for you, do not despair"
At this I pulled myself together
And left the chair where I'd been tethered
My courage came to me at last
I reached the door in one mad dash
I took the steps three at a time
Until I reached the yard outside
I ran up the street then down the lane

**vox poetica**

My legs grew tired, I looked insane
"I must be free by now," I said
"From Edgar Poe, the living dead"
But when I looked behind me then
Old Poe was just around the bend
Above the ground his spectre flew
And as he gained on me it grew
Above the ground his body soared
Crying out for sweet Lenore
Until his countenance did change
Into a Raven large and strange
Before I could begin to scream
Dear Poe became a scary dream
I sat up straight in bed in fright
And turned on every single light
So real was the dream of Poe
It took some time to let it go
Just in case, I checked my mail
Feeling rather week and pale
But as all was just as it should be
To see no ghosts I was relieved
I shut the lid and went to bed
Braved the dark and shed my dread
The next day I would write this down
And steal Poe's poetic crown
Just as I was feeling smug
I felt the blanket being tugged
When I sat up to wrest it free
Edgar Poe stared back at me!

**Trick or Treat With Pets (How My Dog Sees Hallowe'en)**
By Ken Karrer

I just saw Rover from
down the street
beg for something good to eat
(embarrassing really, but)
nothing new about that,
except he did it in a hat
right beside that old Manx cat
named Mephistopheles.
You know the one.
I think he gave me fleas.

Dog sat
Cat spat
Candies flew
Lots to chew

Now that's what I call
Hallowe'en!

**vox poetica**

**Trick or Treat, A Cinquain**
By Mark Gooch

Ghostly
moans and laughter
shadows silently glide
costume-clad boys and girls, eyes wide
sweet treats

**Shhhhh ...**
By Joan McNerney

There is a
witch living
on the corner
where the four
roads meet.

Her eye is
evil, her
nose crooked.

She lays down
the tarot
pattern
with wrinkled
hands.
Asks "do you wish
tea of wormwood
or henbane?"

She will enchant
your mind now
into fields of
wild roses.

vox poetica

### Who Kissed My Neck?
By Gianluca D'Elia

I feel your presence
As it is part of my essence
Though I see no reflection
I sense your pale complexion
And piercing eyes so red
Now tell me the secrets
You've kept for centuries

Vampire in the light beams
Why do you
Have your sights set on
This tasty red drink
A banquet set before you
A fantasy for a creature of the night?

I cannot see your beauty
No matter how hard I try
The ugly never lose
Their ugliness
Empty mirrors shatter
As does my heart

Tell me now, vampire
Why is it you hate me so?
You only wanted me for my blood
Only a lust and a hunger
For me
Vampire in the light beams

From 9/11 to a New Year

At once the morning light shines
And I see you melt away
My heart aches
And rejoices all at once
Colors of silver
Platinum here and there
Shine as I stare
At the vampire in the light beams
For the very last time

Now the question remains unanswered
Who kissed my neck?
But isn't it obvious now?
'Twas the vampire in the light beams of course!

**vox poetica**

**Greedy Ghouls**
By Karen Schindler

Don't open the door
Don't answer the phone
Pretend all together
That no one is home
Evil does stalk
The sidewalk tonight
Amongst tiny beggars
Sweets their delight
They come one by one
Or all in a rush
They ring the doorbell
And wait in a hush
You offer them treats
Hold bated breath in fright
And plead with the gods
No demons tonight

**Jack's Demise**
By Kim Klugh

Our orange globe
with carved-out face
like a lantern flickered
from its porch step place.
Jack glowed at dusk
through his jagged grin,
his visage haunted from deep within.
He cast his spell on passers-by who boldly
looked him in the eye.

October's days are nearly told.
Leaves fly about, the spark's grown cold.
Since the flame burned out Jacks's glow is gone,
his eyes have closed, his face caved in,
there's nothing left of toothy grin.
Even his seeds are now long roasted.
Of his remains—they'll soon be composted.

vox poetica

### La Llorona, The Weeping Woman
By Ray Sharp

¡*Mis hiiiiiiiiijos, mis pobreciiiiiiiiitos!*
My chiiiiiiiiildren, my pooooooooor babies!
The anguished cry from the *arroyo*
pierces the moonless night, a wailing
that emanates from beyond the beyond,
foul ghost-breath on the scruff of my neck,
stink of mud and rot and something worse,
shiver of cold lightening down my spine,
icy hand grabbing me by the *huevos* and
squeezing them like two quail eggs,
a sickening sensation of bony fingers and
the sudden sound of dry brown shells
cracking. Why do you pull me down
to the edge of the black and swirling
waters, oh *La Llorona*, Weeping Woman,
Indian Princess, Traitor of *La Raza*,
*Doña Marina*, *La Malinche*, Wicked
Bitch, Whore of Cortez, Medea-Witch?
You opened our land and your legs
to the false *Quetzalcoatl*, the white-
faced bearded killer who burned the ships
at *Vera Cruz*, and to the ghost soldiers
on their snorting demon-horses who
raped Tenochtitlan and cut out
the beating heart of *México*. And so
you killed your devil spawn, held them
fast under these very waters, and dove
with them, your beloved babies,
swimming to the depths of Hell.

# From 9/11 to a New Year

But you could not kill the *meztizos*,
a million bastard children born of
*Padre España* and *Madre México*.
To this day, you cry from the river
for the flesh of your loin,
for the blood of your heart,
for the pain you endure,
the never-ending curse of filicide,
and the suffering of those who walk
this dry and dusty God-forsaken land.
Down you pull me, under the oily surface
into your muddy lair, your arms like ropes
that bind me tight, your ghost breasts
two empty paper sacks, your sex
a dark and toothless grin that sucks me
with its supernatural attraction
and swallows my soul. Perhaps,
in the end, you had to kill for the shame
your kind have worn since Eve
fell from Grace, the world in a state
of perpetual postpartum depression.
Twice our sins wash down this river,
one time baptism and the other drowning.
I see now that it is only just and good
that I surrender to your sweet embrace
and kiss your dead white lips,
breathe your darkness into my lungs
and join you forever in your watery grave,
wet womb from where we were birthed.
*¡Ay Dios Mío!*

**vox poetica**

**Jersey Boys**
By Bryan Borland

For laughs we dressed
as Jersey girls, gaudy wigs,
earrings that pinched and
Bon Jovi shirts, running between buildings
as the cold weather shook off
its costumed summer with confidence
and I chased you for warmth.
We rang doorbells, a little old
to be beggars in your sister's clothes,
our bags swallowing candy
we poured on your bed afterwards.
You gave me kisses that night,
dozens, wrapped in silver.
I was expecting more.

**Days of the Dead**
By Cassie Premo Steele

I lay out plates of food for the dead
and circle their pictures there, to welcome
back spirits in this cold November air.
I show you your relations, and you wave
like you've seen them before, and I ask you,
Baby, how are they doing, is my uncle
still drinking, is that one still crying,
does this one still like being a nun?
You smile at me, silly, as if to say how human
I am, as if you cannot believe that I
do not know that we are more
than all this, once we are dead.
I pause, shake my head,
try to imagine an alcoholic without his habit,
a nun without hers, a depressed woman
happy and away from her bed.
And then I see that what would remain
would be the mystery that makes people
love a baby, so full of hunger, dying to be fed,
our link back to the beginning, the needful
beat of being that goes on going
long after we all are dead.

# Contributor Series 3:
# Resolution and Resolve

**Resolution 2009**
By Gianluca D'Elia

This year I'll be better at math
And get off my lazy ass
I've been writing too much to realize
That there are formulas I should memorize
It's time to do better, to buckle down
Even though it might make me frown

This year I'll be better at math
I'll follow the correct path
I think I can do it, I just have to try
Maybe my skills will never die.
I'll do better in math this year, you'll see!
Even if I just get a B

**vox poetica**

**Unheard**
By Chris G Vaillancourt

I want the conversations
we'll never have.
The urged words drip
off my tongue
in foreign colours,
and fall to the ground,
unnoticed, unheard.
Ignored are the whispers
from my stained lips.
The words are heard
but remain
unacknowledged.
Around me are a lot
of faces.
Some I recognize and
others I do not.
They smile at me
as they
hold their
conversations.
Talking at me
but never talking
to me.
And despite
the vowels they
pronounce these
faces with their
ears closed
do not hear the

words I return to them.
I want the clouds
to stop turning
grey over my head.
Looking, but not
really seeing the
disappearing self.
With effort I
manage to scream
loud enough to
convince everyone
that
I am still alive.

**vox poetica**

**If I stop to pick up a leaf**
By Sarah Endo

If I stop to pick up
a red-rimmed leaf
with golden heart
I want to revel in that
I don't want anyone to say, *come ON!*
or
*NO, you have to carry that*
*yourself—I can't carry any more*
If I stop to pick up a leaf
brown brittle and small
I don't want you to doubt me:
*Why do you want that leaf?*
(crummy crumbly leaf)
I want you to marvel with me
or
at least allow me to marvel, myself
If I stop upon a heart-
shaped leaf
bold gold and red
If I'm five and find
such a leaf
won't you marvel,
revel too

**Homelessness ... it's real**
By Jimmi Ware-Phillips

They smile to keep from crying out loud
Faceless wandering in the downtown crowd
Trying to regroup from the bittersweet
In need of shelter, a nourishing meal to eat
They are afraid and pretend to be tough
When the truth is being homeless is rough
This is no laughing matter
Please refrain from staring and idle chatter
A child on the streets is no fairy tale
It is a nightmare and we must prevail
Wake up to this painful truth
We must not ignore the exodus of our youth
To err is human, to give is divine
What if that homeless child was yours or mine?
Do something while there still is time

### Recipe for the Impossible
By Cassie Premo Steele

*You must do the things
you think you cannot do.*
—Eleanor Roosevelt

Here is what to do, my friend,
when your blue anger rises
on yourself: Take a break,
take a shower, go walking
in the rain. Do not let
your brain become a monster.
Use your heart to bake a cake,
take it deep into the forest
in winter, and share it
with the birds there.
Listen to the sweetness
of their songs for you.
You must do the things
you think you cannot do,
I tell you. It is the impossible
that will see you through.

**Resolutions**
By Eve Hall

Another year has come and gone.
This is the time we make new goals.
Resolutions that we fail to keep that are,
just another way of lying to ourselves.
Plans to lose weight and not stay up late,
that we will save money and spend less,
and not make our lives a terrible mess.

We will be more peaceable,
and not always feel we're right.
That we will admit to our wrongs,
and try not to fight.

That we will try hard to live and not die,
that we will be truthful and not lie.
That we will love and not hate,
that we will be early not late.

Why do we fool ourselves into making resolutions?
Because we are human.

**vox poetica**

**What Dreams Are Made Of**
By Neil Ellman

Mother dreamed of numbers
not people or lost loves
as the rest of us do
3-7-6
she would announce in the morning
and father would, in the days before
it was legal, place the bet
at the local barber shop.

The night before I was born
she dreamed 2-0-3
and the hospital room had the
very same number—
Good things come in threes,
she said, and the bet was made.
She won, of course,
or that's what she told me
a hundred times.

Father dreamed colors
the kind on jockey silks
and Fridays were our time
to be together at the ponies
are what we called it
me searching for winning tickets
among the discarded dreams
on the grandstand floor
and he studying the racing form
for clues and symbols that

would interpret his dreams
and make them real.
He won, of course,
or that's what he told me
every Friday night.

I still dream of them occasionally
dressed in numbers and motley silks
their dreams and mine
awakened by chance.

### My Uncertain Life
By James G Piatt

Through the broken windows
Of my uncertain life
Summers once glowed warmly
Then faded into the shadows
Of brisk rainy autumns
And barren icy winters

In this unearthly place
Where ravaging ogres tear
Apart my pleasant thoughts
Pounding my happy moments
Into hapless gloom everywhere
I fight the tongueless pain

Of all the mortal slips
Of my joyous youth
That gives dim sorrow
To my lonely thoughts
I still pine for the joyous times
Of pleasant youth and certainty

**Lost Dream**
By Joan McNerney

I am driving up a hill
without a name on an
unnumbered highway.
This road transforms into
a snake winding around
coiled on hairpin turns.
At bottom of the incline
lies a dark village strangely
hushed with secrets.
How black it is. How difficult
to find that dream street
which I must discover.
Exactly what I will explore
is unsure. Where I will find it
is unknown. All is in question.
I continue to haunt gloomy
streets in this dream town
crossing dim intersections.
Everything has become a maze
where one line leads to another
dead ends become beginnings.
Deciding to abandon my search,
I return to my automobile ...
nowhere to be found in shadows.
Finally I look up at the moon's
yellow eye ... my lips forming
prayers to a disinterested god.

### Weathering
By Dee Thompson

My old Mazda slices through the wet cold morning world
Windshield wipers thwock thwock.
I hate driving in rain. Anxiety underlines everything.

The only beauty—tall pines fringing the ashy sky, a fit canopy
to my meditation cave.

Far west, my sister/friend prepares to journey east.

I know her journey.
Years ago I sped across the sky to my children.
Warehoused in orphan prisons, their faces engraved
on my eyelids,
My only thought was Hold on, Mama's coming.

Five years past, my daughter awoke to her first day as an
American.
I cannot forget her—huge eyes, thick straw hair, white stick
limbs,
mute behind her Russian language.
We lived in terror together, Mother and Daughter, bonded only
by paper and mutual longing.

Now we fit together like a pair of old shoes, comfortable from
the long wearing, separate, yet working together.

My son says he misses snow.
We live in a place of rain, a place of tiny winters and lush,
expansive summers.

Studying for a science test, I explain ice wedging to him by recalling the potholes everywhere in Kazakhstan.
I explain about rivers as he remembers the recent torrent in our backyard that swept away our stone angel.
I explain tributaries by showing how fingers connect to hand.
We talk of weathering, of erosion, of alluvial plains, of steep canyons rising from ancient rivers.

I am not a baby! He says indignantly at breakfast. I'm thirteen.

You will always be my baby, even when you have gray hair and a pot belly. My baby. I labored in planes and fell in snow for you.

Time and water change everything.

vox poetica

**I dropped it again**
By Rae Spencer

And of course, it broke
The clap and wrack of it
Familiar as any ruin

Strafed across the floor
As when our parents divorced
In that first long arc of loss

When it whined through the air
Like crystal stroked to cry
And crack

Before the later slap and shatter
Of Daddy's death, the clumsy grief
That fumbles everything fragile

Seamed with glue
Crazed and dull, a grained
Reflective surface

With no memory
Of its molded image, no version
Of itself unscarred, untouched

Only those pieces that fit
Into new shapes, into new lines
Into new hands, which cup and clutch

From 9/11 to a New Day

Though they aren't strong enough
Aren't dexterous enough to keep it
Sealed and safe

But each day determined
To gather the scattered bits
And patch it healed, again

vox poetica

**The Silence of Wind**
By Kay Middleton

Florence wants love,
respect, recognition.
Maybe she even
wants a chance
to start over,
a reincarnation.

She wants to wear the blue
dress with the ecru lace
collar and the peplum
that makes her
look like she has hips
that sway sassy

when she walks, hips
that melt into her
narrow waist.
Her slender frame,
fragile bones,
frail as her spirit.

Florence often travels
in the lane reserved
for left turns, travels
in constant danger
of oncoming traffic
fear filled streets

bordered in prayer.
Her eyes rain
crazy for weeks
supplying moats
of anger and confusion
or the other way 'round?

She contemplates her body;
a maze of blood tunnels,
nerve highways, effervescent scars
scattered on failing flesh
like fish scales on the floor.

Florence fingers a crucifix
on a beaded
gold rope
listens to the silence
of wind,
swallows more pills,
and sleeps.

**The Navigators**
By Joseph Murphy

The buoy rang steadily
As I walked the glade and redwood grove,
That free day of mine.

I paused in a meadow, eyes closed.

Bell in my heart,
Be heard as clearly:
Guide me
And those I love.

# The Contributors

**Anna Alpine** lives and writes in New Jersey, where she is raising 2 children and a bunny.

**Linda Ardison** was born in Fort Smith, AR. Though the granddaughter of a woman who was illiterate, her poetry and fiction have been published in various literary journals in print and online formats including *vox poetica*, *Concerning Poetry*, and *Laurel Review*. Her work has also been included in the anthology *Essential Love: Poems About Mothers and Daughters, Fathers and Sons*. Linda lives in Virginia Beach VA, where she is a member of the Albright Poets, Hampton Roads Writers, and James River Writers.

**Bryan Borland** is a poet from Little Rock, AR. His first full-length collection of poetry, *My Life as Adam*, is available at his website www.bryanborland.com.

**Danielle Cross** writes and publishes in between all the other things that keep her busy day and night. You can see more of her work at her blog http://calliopespen.com/.

**Gianluca D'Elia** is a teenage writer and actor on a quest for world domination (more like outreach of love). He has been writing since he was 9. He is the third youngest contributor to *vox poetica* to date and has also made his name known at *Caper Journal*. In addition to poetry, Gianluca writes songs and he is currently working on a novel called Heal. He is a devoted Kerli fan, a hippie, a singer, and a closeted chocolate addict.

**R Scott DeSena** is 46 years old. He lived in Bergen County NJ until 2004, when he packed up and moved to Boynton Beach, FL, where he currently resides with his daughter Frida, 2 rabbits, Blue and Thumper, and a dog named Sadie. He plays guitar, writes music, writes poetry ... life is good.

**Neil Ellman** lives and writes out of New Jersey. He has been published extensively in national and international print and online journals from A (*Astropoetica*) to Z (*Zygote in My Coffee*), and he has two chapbooks, both dealing with art, to his credit.

**Sarah Endo** is thrilled to be part of the vox poetica community. She lives in Massachusetts with her family, the younger members of which provide her with unbiased feedback such as "You're a good poemer. You should write another one."

**Sandra Forte-Nickenig** is the first-generation American child of two Russian immigrants. Born in Brooklyn, NY, she graduated from Brooklyn College as an English major specializing in the critical analysis of poetry. Her last job before retiring was as an executive for an international self-help group. She has many published articles and reports to her name. Sandra believes there are some feelings that can only be expressed through poetry. Much of her writing explores the immigrant experience, love and loss, and the interconnectedness of man, woman, and nature. She lives in Virginia Beach with her husband. Sandra is a member of the Albright Poets.

**Mark Gooch** has been a paranormal investigator for more than 30 years in the mid-Michigan area. He is currently writing a book on the subject and he has discovered that writing poetry is a great vehicle for word structure and expression.

**Eve Hall** is a self-published author (3 poetry books and 2 children's books) and poet living in Georgia. One of her goals is to publish all of the books she has written for children. She is available for readings and book signings.

**Ken Karrer** is a retired public schoolteacher currently working for the Texas Education Agency. He is a member of Austin Poets at Large and his work has appeared in numerous journals.

**Kim Klugh** is an educator, a freelance writer, and a practicing poet in Lancaster, PA.

**John Lavan** is a poet living in the UK, practicing writing at least 1 poem a day. His passion is words and working through them to feeling. He uses family as a source of inspiration.

**Annmarie Lockhart** is the founding editor of *vox poetica*, an online literary salon dedicated to bringing poetry into the everyday. She has been reading and writing since she could read and write.

**Jean McLeod** lives in Norfolk, VA, where she watches the sun rise over the mouth of the Chesapeake Bay. She is thrilled and amazed that her prose and poetry have been published.

**Joan McNerney**'s poetry has been included in publications such as *Seven Circle Press*, *Dinner with the Muse*, *Blueline*, *63 channels*, *Spectrum*, and Bright Spring Press anthologies. She has read at National Arts Club, SUNY Oneonta, McNay Art Institute, and others.

**Kay Middleton** barely balances on the edge of the sprawling Lake Smith in Virginia Beach, VA, where she writes novels and poetry, the long and short of it. Kay's publishing credits include *Lines & Stars*, *Concise Delights*, *Eat a Peach*, and *vox poetica*.

**Joseph Murphy** is a professional editor and writer living in Michigan. He won the Eisner Prize for Poetry in 1971, UC Berkley's highest award in the arts. He recently began writing again. You can see Joseph's work in journals such as *Living Poets*, *The Tower Journal*, and *Talon*.

**James G Piatt** has been a junior college dean, professor of philosophy, and an administrator of masters programs. He earned his BS and MA from California Polytechnic University and his doctorate from BYU. Retired now, he spends his summers along a river, reading, writing, and penning poetry. His work can be found at *Contemporary American Voices*, *Word Catalyst Magazine*, *Apollo's Lyre*, *Caper Journal*, *vox poetica*, *Shadow Poetry Anthology*, *The Penwood Review*, *Wilderness Review*, *Front Porch Review*, *A Handful of Stones*, and *Autumn Leaves*.

**Sharon Poch**'s poetry has been published in *Moondance*, *vox poetica*, and 2 anthologies. She has won the Christine Sparks award for poetry. A late bloomer, she fell in love with poetry on the cusp of middle age after raising 3 children, a husband, and assorted neurotic pets. Following years of living abroad in Italy and England, she and her naval spouse retired to Tidewater VA, where she pens stories from her heart, poems from her soul. "A loaf of bread, a jug of wine, and my writing friends beside me, singing in the wilderness ... life is good."

**Val B Russell** is a Canadian poet, novelist, and occasional freelance writer. Her work can be found in such diverse places as *Reader's Digest*, *vox poetica*, *Ditch Magazine*, *Referential Magazine*, and *Vwa: Voices for Haiti*, an anthology to aid victims of the earthquake. Val is the author of a middle reader fantasy novel, *The Adventures of Granny Destross and CeeCee*, the first in a series. She is working on an adult novel and a volume of poetry detailing her experiences as a homeless woman.

**Karen Schindler** writes even when she's not writing. A wonderer, a cherisher of life and experiences, she lives with gleeful abandon and pulls others into her wake. Karen's fiction, poetry, and essays can be found at *Eclectic Flash*, *vox poetica*, *WeirdYear*, *Flashes in the Dark*, *Blink/Ink*, *Ink Node*, and *Pill Hill*, *Lame Goat*, and *52 Stitches* anthologies. You can see more of her work at her blog, Miscellaneous Yammering.

**Ray Sharp** is a public health administrator in Michigan's rural, rugged, and remote Upper Peninsula region. His work can be found at *Astropoetica*, *Caper Journal*, *Eclectic Flash*, *Ink Node*, *qarrtsiluni*, *Referential Magazine*, and *vox poetica*.

**Rae Spencer** is a writer and veterinarian living in Virginia. Her poetry has been published in *Poem2Day*, *Willows Wept Review*, *The Driftwood Review*, *Melusine*, *Five Fishes Journal*, and elsewhere. Her work was nominated for a Pushcart Prize in 2009. She can be found online at www.raespencer.com.

**Cassie Premo Steele** is a Pushcart Prize nominated poet, writer, and creativity coach who lives along a beautiful creek in South Carolina. She is the author of 6 books, including a forthcoming novel titled *Shamrock & Lotus*. She is an inspiring guide during the creative process and works with clients in person and long distance. Visit her web site at www.cassiepremosteele.com.

**Dee Thompson** is a writer who lives in Atlanta, GA with her 2 children. She has been writing poetry since she was 5, gaining her first published credit while still in middle school. She holds an MA in creative writing from University of Tennessee. Visit her blog, The Crab Chronicles.

**Chris G Vaillancourt** has had more than 200 poems published in journals in Australia, Canada, Japan, the UK, and the US. He has had a series of chapbooks published by Four Winds Press and his 4th collection of poetry was recently published. He is the founder and editor of the ezine *P&W* http://triangularduck.bravehost.com/.

**Jimmi Ware-Phillips** is a poet with a purpose. She uses her gifts to uplift the hopes of young people in Alaska. She is a Covenant House volunteer for homeless teens. Her organization, Black Feather P.O.E.T.S., works to prevent suicide by producing public service announcements as part of the Reasons to Live campaign. Jimmi loves the beautiful tranquility of living in Alaska and believes in giving back.

www.ingramcontent.com/pod-product-compliance
Lightning Source LLC
Chambersburg PA
CBHW070106100426
42743CB00012B/2667